New Month,
New Moon

To my father who taught me to look at the night sky, and
my mother who put up with all that craziness.
— A.O.

To Guy Bar-Yosef Z"L. We miss you, Brother!
— E.A.

Many thanks to our fabulous astronomy guide Ira Machefsky, the
"Starman of Mitzpe Ramon" www.astronomyisrael.com
A.O. and E.A.

Kar-Ben Publishing
A division of Lerner Publishing Group, Inc.
241 First Avenue North
Minneapolis, MN 55401 U.S.A.
1-800-4-KARBEN

Website address: www.karben.com

Library of Congress Cataloging-in-Publication Data

Ofanansky, Allison.
    New month, new moon / by Allison Ofanansky ; photographed by Eliyahu Alpern.
        pages   cm
    ISBN 978–1–4677–1945–2 (lib. bdg. : alk. paper)
    ISBN 978–1–4677–4670–0 (eBook)
    1. Rosh Hodesh—Juvenile fiction. I. Alpern, Eliyahu. II. Title.
    PZ7.O31New 2014
    [E]—dc23   2013022211

Manufactured in the United States of America
1 – VI – 7/15/14

New Month, New Moon

By Allison Ofanansky
Photos by Eliyahu Alpern

KAR-BEN
PUBLISHING

My family drives along the steep desert road that leads to the Machtesh Ramon canyon. We are going on a camping trip to celebrate Rosh Chodesh, the beginning of a new month in the Jewish calendar.

When we arrive, we meet our guide Ira, who will be leading us on a special hike to learn about the moon.

It is very windy at the rim of the canyon. "Be careful and don't get too near the edge," Ima warns us.

I look through Abba's binoculars. "This evening
we'll look through a telescope," Ira promises.

As we hike along a desert trail, I see an animal with big curved horns. "That's an ibex," Ira tells us. "He must be the abba," I say, "He even has a beard!"

We also see some baby ibexes with small horns.

"The rocks are such pretty colors," Tali says. Aravah puts some of the powdery yellow dirt in her hand and mixes it with water from her canteen to make paint.

She draws crescent moons on Tali's cheeks.

"The moon sets early on Rosh Chodesh," Ira says. "If we want to get a good look, we need to hurry." I watch as he sets up his telescope.

The setting sun turns the canyon red and purple.

A thin curve of moon hangs low in the sky, like a sideways smile.

I stand on a stool so I'm tall enough to look through the eyepiece.
Ira shows me how to adjust the focus.

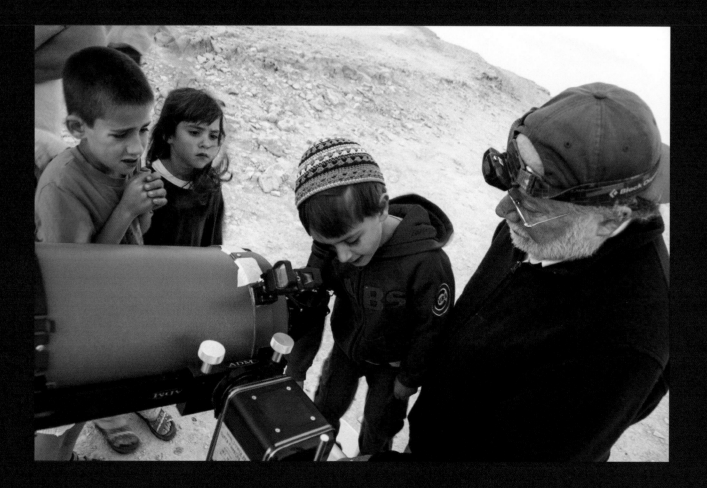

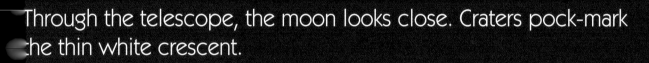

Through the telescope, the moon looks close. Craters pock-mark the thin white crescent.

"Hey, the rest of the moon is there, too!" I say. "I can see it."

"Right," says Ira. "The moon is always the same size, although sometimes it looks big and round, and other times, like tonight, we see just a sliver."

"Why?" I ask.

"Good question. Let's play a little game to help you understand."

By now the sky is dark. Ira lights a lantern on a tripod. "In our game, this will be the sun," he tells us. He blows up a globe and gives it to me and Aravah. "You two hold the earth," Ira says. He gives Shoshana a model of the moon. "The moon doesn't give off its own light," Ira says, "It reflects the sun's light."

Ira tells Shoshana to walk slowly in a circle around us. "As the moon orbits the earth we can see only the part of the moon that is facing the sun," he explains.

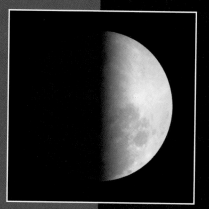

As Shoshana walks around us, I watch the light from the lantern move across the face of the toy moon.

Shoshana stops behind us. "Look at the ball now," Ira says.

I turn.

"What do you see?"

"The moon is all lit up," I answer.

"Right. That's a full moon. We see the full moon when the earth is between the sun and the moon— just like your globe is between the toy moon and the lantern."

When Shoshana stands between us and the lantern I can only see the dark back of the toy moon. "That is what is called the new moon," Ira says. "We can't see any of the lit-up side."

Shoshana takes another step. A sliver of light appears along the edge of the moon model. "Right after the new moon we see a crescent. That signals the start of Rosh Chodesh, a new month in the Jewish calendar," says Ira.

After we finish the game, Ima spreads a blanket on the ground. We lie down and look up at the dark desert sky. Ira uses a strong laser beam to point out stars, constellations, and planets. "I want a laser like that!" I tell Abba.

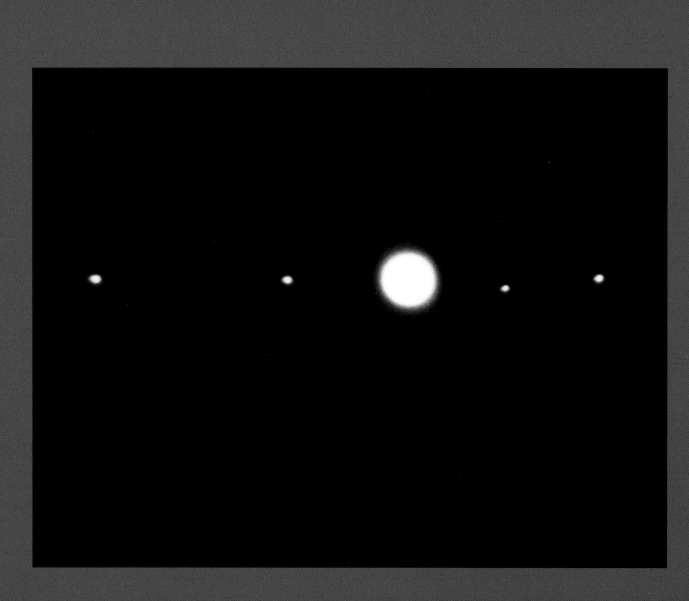

We take turns looking through the telescope again. Ira shows us the planet Jupiter. "If you look closely, you can see four of Jupiter's moons," he says.

"Four moons! How do they know when it's Rosh Chodesh?" I ask.

"There aren't any people living on Jupiter!" Aravah tells me.

I start to get sleepy.
Aravah gives me a
piggy back ride to
the campground.

We pile up sticks in the fire ring,
and Abba lights our bonfire.

As we watch the fire burn Abba tells us, "A long time ago, when the crescent moon of each new month was spotted, the Israelites would announce that it was Rosh Chodesh by lighting huge bonfires on hilltops across the country."

"Time for snacks," Abba announces.
Tali and I help mix up dough and roll out pita bread.

Abba bakes them on the *saj*, a domed metal pan that goes over the fire.

I hold up a pita. "It looks like a full moon," I tell Tali.

Ima opens a jar of chocolate spread. I smear some on half of my pita. "Now it's a half moon," I say.

I cover the rest of the pita with chocolate, leaving only a tiny edge of bread. "Now it's a Rosh Chodesh pita."

Tali and I take big bites of our pita-moons.

"Chodesh Tov!"

"Have a good month!"

PAPER MÂCHÉ MOON

WHAT YOU NEED:

- 1 c. white flour
- Water
- 1 Tbsp. salt

- Newspaper or other scrap paper, torn in strips
- Plastic or styrofoam ball
- White and gray paint

MAKE THE PASTE:

Put the cup of flour in a bowl. Slowly add water and mix until the paste is smooth and about the consistency of pancake batter. Stir in the salt.

COVER THE BALL:

Dip a strip into papier mâché paste. Wipe off extra paste. Lay the paste-covered strip on the ball and smooth it flat. (If you don't want to get your hands messy, you can put the dry paper strip on the ball and paint on the paste with a paintbrush). Continue to add strips of paste-covered paper until the entire ball is covered. Let dry for half an hour. Add another layer and let dry. You can add up to four layers.

MAKE A HANGER OR HANDLE:

To hang your moon model, lay a piece of string against the ball and cover about six inches (15 cm.) with papier mâché. If you are using a styrofoam ball, you can add a handle by pushing a thin stick into the ball.

ADD CRATERS AND MOUNTAINS:

Ridges and craters can be molded out of papier mâché as you add the layers.

PAINT:

When the moon model is completely dry, paint it. Look at pictures of the moon to get an idea of what its surface looks like.

Phases of the moon

First Quarter

Waxing Gibbous

Waxing Crescent

Waning Gibbous

Full Moon

New Moon

Waning Gibbous

Waning Crescent

Last Quarter

ABOUT ROSH CHODESH

Rosh Chodesh, which means "head of the month," occurs when the first sliver of crescent moon appears in the sky, following the new moon. Some Hebrew months have 29 days, others have 30 days. At the end of months that have 30 days, Rosh Chodesh is observed for two days, on the 30th day of the previous month and the first day of the new month. Following months that have 29 days, only the first day of the new month is observed as Rosh Chodesh. In ancient Israel, bonfires were lit on hilltops across the country to announce that a new month had begun. In modern times, the Hebrew calendar has been fixed, so that we know ahead of time when Rosh Chodesh will occur. On the Shabbat before a new month begins, the dates of Rosh Chodesh are announced in the synagogue. On Rosh Chodesh, prayers for the new month are recited. Rosh Chodesh is considered a special day for women, because in Biblical times the women did not offer their jewelry to create the Golden Calf.

ABOUT THE AUTHOR
Allison Ofanansky lives in Israel in the village of Kaditah, near the mystical city of Tzefat, with her husband Shmuel and their daughter Aravah. She enjoys hiking in the hills of the Galilee, where she and her family are involved in many environmental education and "eco-peace" projects. This is the fifth book in her series about Jewish holidays and nature in Israel, including *Harvest of Light, Sukkot Treasure Hunt* (both Sydney Taylor notable books), *What's the Buzz: Honey for a Sweet New Year,* and *Cheesecake for Shavuot.*

ABOUT THE PHOTOGRAPHER
Born and raised outside Chicago, Eliyahu (Andy) Alpern has been interested in food, travel, and photography since early childhood. He lives in Tzefat, Israel. Specializing in 360-degree panoramic images of Israel, Eliyahu's images include breathtaking shots of holy sites, markets, and natural vistas. To experience more of his art, visit www.tziloom.com. This is his fifth book with author Allison Ofanansky.